ECONOMICS

AN OUTSIDER LOOKING IN

SAMRIDHHI MANDAWAT

For readers like you!

Contents

Preface

We need many more to work in this area of social science, especially in developing countries like India, where the study of economics is seen as the pursuit of the elite or a minimum recourse to graduate study in commerce. The subject deserves the attention of a large number of young scientific minds of a given generation that have grown to believe that technology and engineering are the end-all of academics!

While the chapters themselves are laid out as they occurred to the author, it is hoped that you will find a thread of cogency in them. The last chapter is named the conclusion. The nature of this chapter is quite unknown at this time of the draft.

But no writer of non-fiction wants to write more than a dozen pages without wanting to summarize its essence, so if you are the impatient one like me, perhaps you can skip straight to the end and it might save you time!

Happy Exploring!
Samridhhi Mandawat

Acknowledgements

༒༒༒

Dr. Nausheen Nizami
Associate Professor (Economics)
Department of Social Sciences
School of Liberal Studies - PDEU

༒༒༒

Mr. Naresh Iyer
Dy. Manager - Bharat Electronics Ltd.
Former Assistant Vice President - Mahindra Satyam

༒༒༒

1
introduction

To an outsider looking in, on the over-arching subject of economics, one is either curious about the contents, looking forward to breakthroughs, or merely dismissive about the subject, as a whole.

"To come very near true theory and to grasp its precise application are two very different things as the history of science teaches us. Everything of importance has been said before by somebody who did not discover it."

- A. N. Whitehead

With that disclaimer, we can still say that there would be hardly any soul on earth who is not affected by this fascinating subject, especially if some form of societal contact is retained in the life of an individual.

While at one end of the spectrum, we imagine that the billionaires (aided by their astute financial advisors) that straddle our imaginations and the fronts of our newspapers are extremely informed of the subject, at the other end, we place students that are perhaps trying to comprehend the various nuances of this subject to make a living at the end of their select programs.

Perhaps, this book may fall short of the expectations of both. Then, whom should this book interest? The economists? Some of them, who already consider themselves aware, at least of this subject if not of all subjects, as they pretend to show on popular market watch shows of the TV or the streaming net these days?

Well, having very briefly established that all humans are affected by this subject despite their relative interests in how it governs their destinies, the readership of this monograph is then like the electromagnetic spectrum, where only a small portion is discernable to the human eye.

Given this spectrum of readership, there must be something in it for those running economies of nations and those running a household – at least in terms of understanding if not in terms of decision-making abilities. Though, we might expect that the former, that is, understanding, is in some way connected to the latter, the ability to decide.

Herein, also enters the nebulous subject of choice. It is this interesting mix of understanding, choice, and decision making that makes economics at once a subject on which everyone has an opinion. Though we may dismiss opinions through the popular retort that references are an unmentionable part of the human anatomy, we inadvertently admit that opinions are as important in directing the dynamics of an economy as that vital part of the excretory system to the human body.

This brings us to next aspect that economists tend to wax eloquent (no pun intended) on here, that is, communication – perhaps, no other subject lends itself to miscommunication as much as economics does and some inquiry into why this is so might be interesting to the accused-in-chief of this book, the wannabe economist!

Now, a natural question arises, how are economists different in this regard (they are being accused of involving themselves in subjects that they do not specialize in) from say, engineers or artisans, and maybe stay-at-home spouses?

Because their theories and decisions touch the lives of people the world over. The aesthetic of a painting or the heating of a microwave oven doesn't touch people in general, and surely not in the negative unless it is put through the vagaries of the economic process. This puts an unjustified responsibility on the economists which is usually not associated with any other profession.

This unjustified responsibility comes into stark contrast when the same is linked with the lifestyles of the practitioners of the most vocal of this class - the bankers!

Also, it brings into focus the major mode of operation of the economic process – transaction. In that sense, the human aspect dominates over the machine, thus economics causes the focus to shift from the problem of automation to the problem of the transaction! The fallout then is that for every economic process we are forced to focus on humans rather than the process! This makes the subject both controversial and error-prone when it comes to its practice!

The other major actor in the economic process is the customer or the consumer. Two closely aligned designations for perhaps the same notion but the latter with a largely pejorative tinge which implies that all forms of consumption are perhaps at somebody else's cost!

Thus, some sort of a relationship between the customer or consumer and the other stakeholders in an organization or against a backdrop becomes necessary as a guiding pathway if we are to talk about that economics that may be hitherto unknown to the economists!

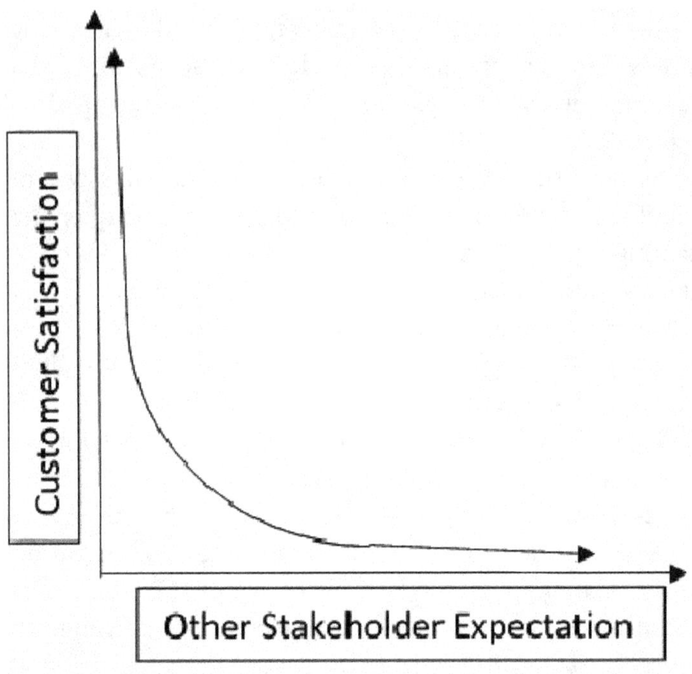

Figure 1 - Reproduced from memory. Inspired by: Mr. Teotia, ex-Director, Bharat Electronics, during a lecture on TQM at MDI, Gurgaon, India

The following figure perhaps very well recognized from its pattern resemblance to many such graphs in various subjects, typically the 'Kano Diagram', then, forms one such guiding pathway to the line of thought espoused in this book. The difference is that it is a 'rotated' pattern and the axis titles are different to lend a slightly different flavor in the context of the subject of this book. Since the vertical axis is the same, one only needs to give reasons for the dependence of its shape on the other parameters that might constitute the horizontal axis in the context of the economic process.

Among the stakeholders involved in the economic process, the customer needs to be separated because they are the recipient of the active involvement of other stakeholders in the process. Thus, a metric related to their satisfaction forms the ordinate or 'y-axis', denoted CS in figure 2. The expectation of the other stakeholders, denoted OSE, automatically forms the abscissa or the 'x-axis'

The 'hyperbolic' nature of the curve can be understood by the fact that if this 'curve' is to apply to all types of organizations then this shape seems to be an intuitive fit.

To the far left of the curve, we might imagine organizations that are high on customer satisfaction but where the stakeholder expectations are very low. The extreme cases of this type could be the "Sisters of Charity" kind of altruistic organization, commonly associated with Mother Teresa or even a group of sannyasins commonly found in all corners of India.

At the extreme right, one might expect to include 'monopolistic' businesses or even pirates in the extreme whose consideration for an entity by name of a 'customer' may be next to non-existent, while their expectations from their engagement might be close to infinity!

Thus, we see in one graph, how the entire economic process as applicable to every individual or group may be placed.

In keeping with the times, one may envisage that a 3rd dimension or the 'z-axes' may be added to this curve.

This will cause the curve to morph into a sheet, which warps, from the bottom corner of a 'box' to an ellipse/circle that is drawn with the body diagonal connecting one adjacent corner to its counter-part on top as a diameter, while retaining its secular character to all three axes!

An umbrella surfaces – this 3rd dimension might incorporate an inverse climate change metric or an environmental sustainability metric denoted ES in figure 3.

Again, one might envisage the value for "monopolists" or the other stakeholder expectations (OSE) being perceived with no concern about the environmental impact at the far end of their axis and the "saints", again seeing their value at a minimum completely parallel (that means to the benefit of) to "other axis" on the customer satisfaction (CS) – environmental sustainability (ES) plane, or the CS-OSE plane, that is, with the minimum value for their selves!

(See figure 2 for better visualization)

However, for most of us that are less mathematically inclined the photo of an umbrella with its top pointing downwards at the origin of the cardinal coordinate system shown in figure 2, with all points on its surface equidistant from each plane, is sufficient to rouse our imagination, –

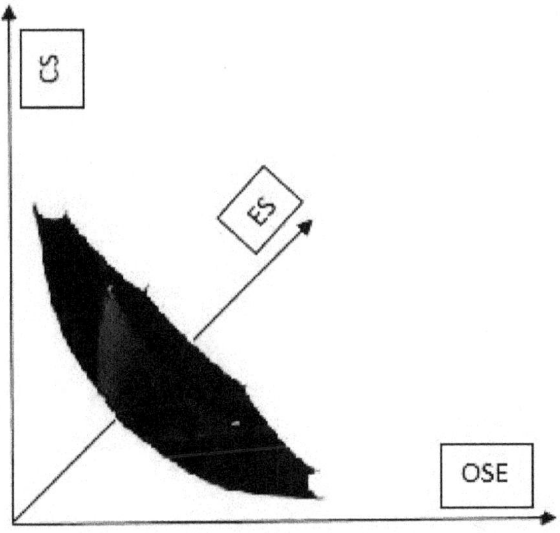

Figure 2: An Umbrella surface oriented to point to the origin of a 3-D Orthogonal Coordinate System.

A slight strain on the grey cells to delve into the associated mathematics of the surface of an umbrella (cloth portion only) will tell us how complicated the subject of economics itself is about the intellectual spectrum of anyone economist as attempted to be described here.

The author, ad nauseum, does not claim to educate the entire community on the subject. What is intended is just to open one's mind-space up to any ideas of local integrations which, when stitched together, it is hoped will serve larger and larger portions of humanity without clash and with minimum impact on the environment.Whatever this book might not do, it would be a good primer to many high school graduates with a background in calculus to opt for economics with its references to a lot of buzzwords that we all hear about.

2
loss of continuity and consequent loss of basis

The basis of modern economics is undoubted, the mathematics of calculus. There is a simple basis to calculus that tends to get forgotten as we navigate through its massive superstructure. A superstructure whose foundations were laid by Sir Isaac Newton or Gottfried Leibniz centuries ago, notwithstanding the controversy as to who was the first to lay it.

Sir Isaac Newton also established the link of calculus to economics by linking it to the paper currency of England as the Warden of the Royal Mint through the availability of gold reserves.

Thus, gold – a real commodity, currency – a medium for the exchange of goods and services, was given a basis for calculation in mathematics through the subject of calculus.

However, over centuries the most recurrent check of the basis of calculus, as applicable to the subject of economics (or for that matter any subject) seems to be forgotten leading to regular failure of otherwise common-sense predictions.

This basis of calculus is what is called a "Continuum".

The word calculus, itself means a small pebble, as most of us who have experienced the horrific pain of a kidney stone and tried to figure what this word was doing in their medical report, would know! Now, in mathematics, this small pebble represents the piece in another counting instrument of yore attributed to the Chinese, the abacus!

Cut to high school mathematics, one is hardly explained how this discrete pebble which we used for counting numbers as kids if we ever did, coalesces into the continuous substratum for computing the area of a piece of paper or portion of land or even the geometry of 3-dimensional space!

The key here is the word "Continuum" or the concept of continuity where we assume that whatever area or volume, we are calculating is a larger number of very tiny pebbles!

Thus, tiny particles of paper, form the continuous sheet of paper that allows us to use calculus to compute the area of an irregular piece of paper, no matter how much it is folded or warped.

Thus, economists can use the mathematics of calculus to compute areas of the surfaces of complex figures as shown in figure 2 and interpret its results in terms of the components of the principal axes. This allows them to comment on the effect of a portion of the area of the concerned surface on the entity represented by the axes, namely, the customer, the other stakeholders, or the environment!

But what if there is no "Continuum"? Is the concept of continuity and its associated mathematics of continuity and its associated mathematics of calculus still valid for economics?

What constitutes a lack of continuity for economics? Is this taught in Basic Calculus?

The above questions become very relevant when we see TV debates, especially in India, where knowledgeable economists are pitted purposely against articulate political party spokespersons while discussing the state of the economy!

The scenarios that unfold are as follows: a smart political party spokesperson misguides a large number of 'so-called' traders against the proper analysis of well-meaning and learned economists. Thus, misinformation, rather than knowledge, becomes the basis of trade.

A blinded-by-animus but a well-reputed economist can arouse an entire country to rebellion by putting forward well-argued theories which incorporate this slip about lack of continuity in the associated math!

A cacophony of supporters between these extremes allows for entertainment in the name of debate and worse still such cacophony governs the destiny of nations!

The purposeful misreporting of data and data collection methodologies has been avoided in the above scenarios as that has greater relevance to communication and political stratagem than the understanding of, where, lack of basis misguides even the learned!

To get back to our analogy, a lack of continuity implies a hole or holes in the umbrella, this means a whole lot of water (in this case, money) can leak in or out and be siphoned to personal gain. A relationship which we might be able to connect with a later chapter on the rich and the nature of their richness!

So, the first thing that the author learned to ask, to understand the subject of economics, was, 'What is the nature of continuity in the subject of economics?' Some idea of the nature of continuity would help us realize where it breaks down so one is at least alerted when a statement to the contrary is made, all mathematics notwithstanding!

The clue comes from one's ability to understand subjects through words! And again, the keyword here is Transaction! Economics is economics because it deals with the subject matter of transactions. If human beings lived as self-sufficient beings on earth without transacting with one another, the whole subject of economics would have no reason for existence!

Thus, the best definition of economics that one can arrive at is that - It is a subject that allows one to calculate the net effect of single or bulk transactions in the continuous space of its medium of exchange!

In a barter, there is no medium of exchange! There is only an exchange of goods and services. The transaction brings an end to the continuity and the continuous space is called wealth! Now, compare this with the standard definition of Economics given by the last word in Economics of the 20th century, Paul A Samuelson –

> "*Economics is the study of how men and society choose with or without the use of money, to employ scarce productive resources, which could have alternative uses, to produce various commodities over time and distribute them for consumption, now or in the future, among various peoples and groups in society.*"

[P.A. Samuelson, Economics, An Introductory Analysis, 7th Edition (New York: Mcgraw-Hill,1955)]

The intellectual problem of the author is that the above definition does not link the subject to its origins which is briefly stated next.

It is the strong conjecture of the author that what Sir Isaac Newton did centuries ago was to lay mathematical foundations for manipulations in this continuous space, by creating a medium of exchange on paper, currency, or money, as the Warden of the Royal Mint for the Queen (or King of England)!

A sort of treaty between the state and another state or any individual or group of citizens of any transacting pair governed by that state!

And now the link to the definition of Prof. Samuelson becomes clear.

History books cruelly hide this fact by stating that Sir Isaac Newton, a bachelor all his life, pursued the strange practice Alchemy – the science or magic, depending on one's disposition, of transmuting base metal to gold – towards the end of his life portraying him as a crass materialist, which, he very well might have been given other facts of his controversy with Gottfried Leibniz!

By bringing the math of calculus to the net effect of bulk transactions, he veritable converted paper (wood) to gold. A task that the legendary Merlin might have been proud of! Those of us with a lesser understanding thought it to be reversed, converting the gold to paper, till some smart economists repealed the 'gold standard' set in motion by Sir Isaac Newton in the economic game. (The web informs that 15 August 1971 was the date when President Nixon changed the dollar/**gold** relationship to $38 per ounce. He no longer allowed the Fed to redeem dollars with **gold**.)

An interesting development which we hope lay the soul of Sir Isaac Newton to rest at least with regards to economics and the destinies of nations!

While paper money continues to play a great role in economics, and the rise of digital currency, credit cards and such, including the crypto variety, threatens its existence; the calculus of Newton and Leibniz might not go away so easily as the basis of economics because they inspire a world-view that is very difficult to replace without an upheaval in all humanity.

It has got to do with the nature of conservation laws and the notion of equality that niggles the best of minds both philosophically and as a matter of physics. More about this in the chapter related to Technology.

So, lack of the basis of calculus, that is lack of continuum, is the first involuntary response that the mind of a beginner in economics must be trained to detect! This will help the economist to know when to stop calculating (can you see the homonymous relationship to calculus?) and start observing the human ends of the transaction or transactions or transactional process and processes.

3

individual choice doesn't aggregate to consumer behaviour

The most ubiquitous concept in economics involves two players – a supplier and a consumer.

The supplier supplies good and services and the consumer consumes. The background where many such suppliers and consumers interact is called the market, where both transact at a mutually agreed price using the medium of exchange (currency) for the given quantity of goods or services. The following diagram is the most popular beginning point of all economics textbooks:

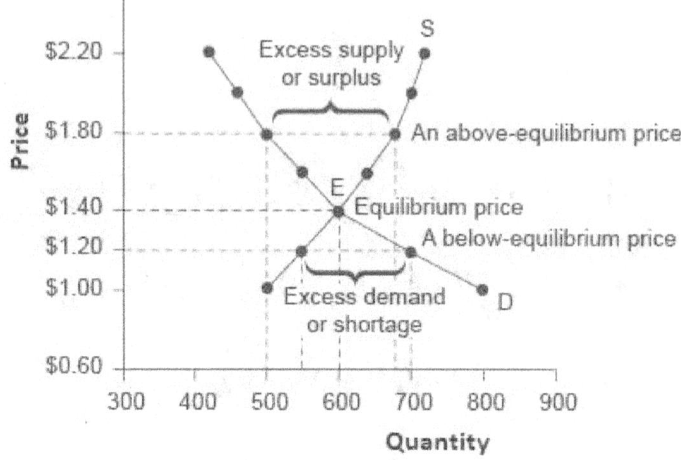

Figure 3 - the diagram is called the demand and supply equilibrium diagram and the word equilibrium has some significance.

Again, the most important underlying conditions for the use of this diagram are reiterated in textbooks but quite forgotten when it comes to practice! Some of the conditions are worth recollecting just so that our minds build in an automatic alert mechanism against their violation –

1. Time and spatial limits must justify the treatment of goods (and services (?)) as a commodity.
2. The goods (and services (?)) are completely uniform, meaning they are of the same quality and have a uniform price!

The demand function shown by the curve 'D' in the figure above, is a function that records for each possible price of the given product (singular for goods) or service, the total quantity that the buyers would choose to purchase. Thus, Individual choice is a very important factor in knowing demand! Think of it as the pebble we discussed that coalesces into a substratum or sheet – similarly individual choice is a discrete entity that coalesces into an aggregated quantity represented by the demand function.

But this aggregation is not straightforward even if the complicated math of partial derivatives is followed because as a community, consumers of the same good or service do not behave like any one of them might.

Thus, the title is very apparent even if we look at ourselves concerning a particular commodity as a consumer, say, cereal-like rice, and see the pattern of our behavior. The vagaries of human behavior then take over the hidden principle of rationality that we have superimposed on our theoretical consumer. Naturally, we aggregate this we don't find a fit to any mathematical function and the bottom falls out of the most revered diagram in the history of economics!

No wonder then that the Nobel Prize in Economics which initially went to mathematicians/statisticians has now started alternating between them and behavioral psychologists!

The laypersons then are hardly bothered and a whole community of middle to top-level executives lead extremely stressed-out lives, earning lots of money for peddling their versions of the demand for their organizations produce even though management schools do their best to teach them consumer behavior through 'utility-maximizing consumer' models and its real-life limitations!

However, all is not lost for the world has enough pockets where homogeneity of products and enforced regulation allow mathematical models to operate in aggregating individual choice into the larger aspect of Consumer Behavior.

The study of the breakdown conditions then in smaller and larger of such pockets gives opportunity to both academics and market opportunists to forge ahead with their respective goals!

So, the readers are encouraged to read their textbooks to the 'T' and those in business must know their consumers' choice almost individually as only then they will be able to come up with a demand function that is the sum of rationally (sub) groupable aggregates.

Thus, there seem to be a few major intellectual formations on this subject –

Study of psychology to know all about a particular individual preference, which can then be summed up for many such individuals representing that psychological stereotype to aggregate demand. Conditions that allow such aggregation and those that disallow such aggregation concerning each particular good or service.

Is price quantized for the particular product or is the Quality-Cost (Price) curve infinitely continuous? And then back to serial numbers one and two for knowing the demand? Meaning, for example, is the smartphone market existent at different price levels, or does the market for simple mobile phones still exist, if so, are they varying continuously separated by a price bandgap?

The problem is that except for the third, which in turn is dependent on 1 and 2, the settled theory of calculus doesn't apply!

This is both an opportunity and a pitfall for the subject of economics.

Opportunity to explore the final frontier of all sciences, the human mind! After all, throughout history, economics has been the biggest driver of research, isn't it?

Pitfall because the tendency to slip into non-traditional modes of evaluation may be the undoing of the very subject which is known to cause severe strife the world over in the past. It is now perhaps established that economics is a very clear indicator of the onset of war-like conditions in any given part of the world.

The Two World Wars have enough data on this for all mankind to take the subject seriously enough! The choice is a funny word for it encompasses the concepts of desire and freedom in one word.

In the context of economics, one can be regulated – freedom can be regulated – that too, in given boundaries. But what does one do about desire?

It is here that the mysteries of the unknown tend to influence the destinies of mankind through knowledge (of given topics).

Once we understand this, then we are on the lookout for what aspect of any mathematics models these concepts or includes them in its assumptions. Then, we can interpret the results of the math or no its limitations correctly. The beauty is that this aspect of economics is a matter of interest both to the housewife and the Central Banker and everyone in between.

A lot of money is devoted to stoking desire. Is there perhaps better use for that money? One can't argue or can argue either way. Thus, the germ of desire, engulfed in the shell of choice lures the divers of the marketplace!

One can always stand on the seashore and observe the process or better still admire the pearls on the neck of a pretty maiden but that has as much impact on the economics of demand and supply as the TV anchor has in predicting the result of the next baseball or cricket game – entertainment value only!

One of the professors of the author, when asked, which should be the minimum subjects taught to a student so that they are fit for the world, replied – Economics, Calculus, and one ancient language! The author would like to modify that list marginally to rephrase it as – Psychology, Calculus, and one ancient language. (Which is a quiet personal opinion.)

Would these encompass the basics of understanding, choice, decision-making, and communication as enunciated in the Introduction, for economics as a subject, to be completely relevant in the human transactional space?

Undoubtedly, for understanding and choice would be covered under Psychology, the math of decision-making under the regime of Calculus and the Ancient language would help one correct transmission errors when this knowledge is communicated through Time.

4

technology creates its market

❦

A professor once explained to me the difference between science and technology and it stuck. Natural laws are science, its application is technology. Thus, when we see the application of mathematics to explaining nature, we understand that we are in the domain of science and when we use mathematics to derive utility out of natural laws then it is technology.

A wheel, then, is the most remarkable and enduring technological breakthrough! Any study of the history of economics would be incomplete without the impact of this breakthrough in affecting the transactions of human civilization from that point in time. In modern times, this word, technology has come to be grossly abused to relate to only the software part of any development, as if all that is there to be explored on the hardware side has already been explored! And, not without cause. The fact is any improvement in hardware is related to breakthroughs in sciences related to materials or the state of matter. Successive leading physicists have suggested that for the last half of a century, there has been no dramatic breakthrough in the world of physics after the agreement on the Standard Model of Particle Physics.

Since almost 1970, we have been only conducting experiments to prove all that has been already anticipated. The Higgs Boson of the Multi-Billion-dollar experimental setup at CERN, Europe, the equally costly LIGOs (Laser Interferometer Gravitational-Wave Observatory) in the US, and similar facilities in smaller scales all over the world are eloquent testimony to mankind's investment in a quest for furthering the boundaries of knowledge rather than extending the utility of that very same knowledge to all members of its kind!

The recent article "Why the foundations of physics have not progressed for 40 years" by Sabine Hossenfelder, in the online news magazine, Changing How the World Thinks, Issue 84, 8 January 2020, or the more published book "The Problem with Physics" by a famous scientist-writer Lee Smolin gives us abundant ammunition to defend this starting position on technology.

No wonder that technology has pushed forth on the software side to bring out more utility before the discovery of new laws of the material universe throw open further avenues for exploitation. Silent slow background gnawing away in terms of hardware improvement as demonstrated by Moore's law in the field of semiconductors is different from the breakthroughs of Nuclear, Laser, and Vacuum Technologies that dominated the first half of the nineteenth century.

Nevertheless, the markets have continued to rule the roost, in fact allowing failed astrophysicists to try their hands in the equally challenging field of economics by allowing them to create complex models of how markets operate. Their understanding of the complexity of the Universe was expected to allow street smart managers to use their modeling expertise with a large number of variables to place bets in tradeable entities based on the calculus of mathematics which we have talked about so much. The fact that many of them work on inside information and the astrophysicists or brilliant mathematicians are mere 'bodies' on the show to justify some of the large costs that are passed off in their names is the dirty secret that our society allows in its hypocrisy, to persist in the name of intellectual hubris!

Now, how does technology create its market? The answer to this is like the gorilla in the room! Just follow any technology over its lifecycle and you see how technology is that snake in Kekule's dream that feeds on its tail!

An interesting example comes from the author's own experience in the development of a medical laser for the posterior capsulotomy. Posterior Capsulotomy or Posterior Capsular Opacification (PCO) is a simple procedure of removing a film that grows behind the artificial lens that is put in place after a cataract operation. Now, because an artificial lens is put in place, the surgeons must leave some tissue in the eye to 'anchor' the lens! The human body then causes this tissue to grow and hold the lens. But, soon enough a film is formed either in front of the lens or behind the lens or on both sides depending on the efficacy of the surgeon.

A necessity of a second surgical operation arises on an already elderly patient which is resolved in a few seconds if it is a PCO by firing a laser into a small pool of liquid behind the lens called the aqueous humor. The blast in that small space creates waves to puncture the film which then retreats to the periphery of the lens and then doesn't grow again or grows over 15 plus years. The whole procedure of posterior capsulotomy takes a few seconds and the patient walks in and walks out.

Thus, the relatively modern technological procedure of most cataract operations (the nationalist votaries of the Ancient Indian method described by Sushruta is the 5th Century AD may kindly pardon me) by Phaco-Emulsion - a default procedure for cataract these days - almost invariably creates the market for the lasers made to resolve PCO! Technology creates its market!

Closer to daily experience, anybody that has lost data and paid companies to get it recovered would know that computer viruses are the manifestation of technology creating their market. When you deal in something in software that you know is going to store, manipulate or transact with data dear to a customer at a very higher level, then you inject a 'vulnerability' during the creation of the software. Later, you sell a solution to the same customer by smartly pointing out that vulnerability either through an 'ethical hacker' or through straightforward threats issued anonymously so that the customers are forced to seek refuge in anti-virus software which are probably held by the same creators of the original software.

An ugly manifestation of technology creating its market!

The final aspect that links technology to economics through markets is the domain of energy. Energy needs represent a growing demand at all points in the known history of mankind! One of the indicators of 'regional peace' according to the author when seen throughout the history of the world might be the differential distribution of per capita demand for energy. The lower it is, in absolute value, in any region, the more peaceful that region is likely to be! And if the differential crosses a certain threshold between two close regions, then acrimony is bound to arise!

One of the key drivers of the modern state of the economy world over is the distribution of the energy basket of every nation in terms of its energy source. Going forward this will be an abiding aspect of economics and technology will be the key differentiator in the bridge between the double E – Energy, and Economics!

Now, if we put two and two together and see that the nature of technology is to create its markets and combine it with the ever-growing need for energy per capita we are immediately prodded towards what we can call the engine of growth for a nation.

In other words, those countries that suffer from a demand slump should immediately look at the composition of their energy basket and look at means by which demand for lower forms of energy can be transformed to demand higher forms of energy!

Now, a basic course in thermodynamics will tell us that heat is a lower form of energy as compared to electricity, which itself is a lower form of energy as compared to work!

Work (Energy) being defined as Force times the distance moved by the object on which the force is applied in a linear direction!

Now, in the lighter vein, the joke in engineering always is –

F (Force) = M (mass) x A (acceleration)

Work = F x D (displacement)

Work = M x A x D = MAD

People with engineering backgrounds must have been truly MAD (pun) studying all this, while what Economists do is to treat work as a pseudonym for employment! (Harsh, but true!)

Thus, when lower forms of energy are moved to higher forms of energy, more 'effort', or 'work' is required as per the 2nd law of thermodynamics. Simply translated, it means more employment!

The economists are right, the language is consistent with the math. Thus, if old thermal power stations are to be replaced by new solar power stations, there will be a growth in employment opportunity, maybe of a different skill, which in turn will put more incomes in the hands of people which in turn will spur demand growth in the economy. On the supply side, of course, it will ease the energy supplies and the calculus of supply-demand equilibrium will affect the preferred goods that a nation lives on.

Taking the economics of energy discussions, at the global level in the context of technology and the backdrop of the Customer-Stakeholder- Environment matrix that we saw in the Introduction, we see how crucial the energy basket of every country is in determining trade negotiations. How various countries leverage their relative advantages sometimes in the name of the environment, sometimes in the name of development, and other times by sheer intransigence without anybody having the humility to admit that this complexity is perhaps too much to be even handled by the combined intelligence of all mankind!

The umbrella surface is stretched by too many factors as each country tries to maximize those that portions of the surface that allow the net effect of bulk transactions to move positively for them.

Intellectual positions then are only political with hardly any base in common undisputed knowledge! Yet, the environmentalists will have a holier than thou attitude, and Greta Thurnbergs of the world will lecture to the leading economists and political leaders of the world, who will in the most unpalatable display of hypocrisy nod in public and renege on all agreements once they are back in their countries to ratify the accords with their respective representatives of the people!

Meanwhile, technology-led by the individual quest for excellence will work in local markets seeking a price equilibrium of demand and supply shown in the figure at the start of Chapter 2, till sufficient success or scale starts to attract punters seeking to make money on money through sheer speculation in the stocks that trade on these specific technologies.

Thus, we see that technology creates, manipulates, and perhaps destroys markets in recurring cycles of economic buoyance and depression touching the lives of the individual and the collective, through war and peace, through winter and summer, in an all-powerful, omnipresent existence that is more reminiscent of a central figure in religion than a product of science which it is!

5
the K shape

We have often heard, about the economic gap – the rich becoming richer and the poor, poorer. (But to extend this, not necessarily poor!)

First, let us start at the beginning and try to agree on what we mean by rich or poor. Any person who has extra wealth over and above that which is required by them to support themselves and their dependents in keeping with an acceptable standard of living by their expectations can be called rich.

It is the disposal of "extra wealth" that distinguishes the truly rich and the defined rich. As to the poor, they need to first check their expectations and then seriously adapt in today's world because too many people are piggybacking on their definition to their detriment!

First, let us focus on the rich and see how they get richer. There are books galore on this as to how somebody made their millions, etc. The popular 'Rich Dad Poor Dad' by Robert Kiyosaki promoted by everyone associated with the network marketing group called Amway, is one such and not read by the author. However, the summary of it as conveyed to the author is that 'royalty' as a regular source of income is one way to keep getting rich!

This probably is one of the temptations that drive many patents and other intellectual properties but is surely not the root cause in the opinion of the author. The rich, not necessarily being the most knowledgeable, is perhaps the quickest recognizers of new knowledge and information!

This means that they are wired to be always 'in touch' and to spot what is likely to be slightly and sufficiently ahead of the curve than their counterparts of the economy. The next thing of course is their deployment of the extra wealth at their disposal to either exploit a loophole in regulation or manipulate regulation in a manner to preserve their knowledge/information supremacy.

Is this cheating? Perhaps, but that is how societies have functioned since history and the sooner the economist comes to terms with this fact, the better they get at understanding the subject and achieving their personal and professional goals.

But a little more here about knowledge and information. The traditional movement in this domain is Data-Information-Knowledge- Wisdom.

You will see that though the rich constantly talk of data and extol the virtues of wisdom, what they are interested in is only information and knowledge and perhaps in that order strictly as it tells them a priority to their actions in how to constantly keep churning their disposable wealth to higher and higher quantum levels!

The other corollary to this line of thought is – The knowledgeable are never poor! Incredible as it sounds, the reason for the focus on education among a certain class of people in India and China, notably their native ability with numbers, has got to do with this genetic societal memory that knowledge and wealth are natal linked!

The very rich then hand a social advantage down their generations which cannot be measured by the extra wealth that they leave for their next few generations. One must also consider the impact of the genetic memory of this urge to shield oneself against poverty by courting some or other form of learning!

Even when we look at those that have wasted their lives in an opulent display of the excess wealth of their previous generation, we find that they eventually settle down to consolidate their possessions for it takes successive generations to squander away the earning of one in peaceful times at a nominal rate without a genetic course correction kicking in!

The most striking cases of the rich becoming poor are usually found in the same generation where a sudden increase in wealth has not equipped the person with the wherewithal to take responsible measures to safeguard it for a future generation if there is one.

In the US, one hears of an exorbitantly high rate of Inheritance Tax that is a societal measure to bring a sense of equity to this observation that has no doubt been noted since the French Revolution.

Naturally, ways around it too have been worked out in terms of the creation of foundations to which the next of kin are appointed as trustees or guardians allowing them in a sense both – (a) freedom to choose their mode of wealth creation; as well as (b) to provide them a security cover for the minimum essentials that their erstwhile lifestyles might have afforded.

Countries like India, with a colonial past, have an enormously complicated regulative structure on income and wealth making one wonder about the collective intelligence of its natives, even as the nation approaches 75 years of Independence.

The income divide – a favorite metric of the economists – is then quite misleading from this point of view because it doesn't consider the subjective notion of a standard of living. A farmer smoking his version of tobacco on a coir matted cot in rural Gujarat, a rich state in India, might be the owner of a few Audi cars and the Chairman of the largest bank in the same country might not be a close second. A comparable dataset simply doesn't exist, circumstantial evidence however does bear out this analogy, with all apologies to an organization popular by the name of Forbes!

For all their cunning, the British are the ones that have most grasped this concept and it is reflected in their devising the starting positions of the 1 mile, now 1500m race!

An ideal economy reset must have a regulative regime or a tax structure that reflects this starting position with a merging into a common lane at a future point in time when all the citizens of a nation are said to have reached a minimum acceptable standard of living! If wishes were horses...

There would need to be precise measurement processes and an army of accountants, computer engineers, or at least software programmers working on an economic model built by some well-meaning mathematical minds!

Now, let us come to the other side, that of the poor. If the previous generation has been poor, then the expectations of the standards of living are automatically adjusted for the present generation to target their financial goals so that they qualify for what they might call rich by the agreed definition.

But what if the previous generation or one of the earlier generations was rich, perhaps truly rich, and circumstances caused a drastic change in fortunes – the expectations of a generation would change mid-life and unnecessarily high levels of relative standard of living compared to others in society would be set. Not only that, stories of it would have been passed along in place of tangible inheritance. Yet, the biggest takeaway is that the succeeding generation would surely bet on knowledge as an insurance investment somewhere down the line! This knowledge need not be academic in fact in most cases it is not. It is a transfer of skills.

Perhaps, the biggest threat to the rich and the poor in the future is that the development of Artificial Intelligence and Machine Learning limits the scope of this transfer of skills for the vast majority for whom it is the only real, life insurance policy. It forces generations into the systematic acquisition of scientific knowledge that only modern (western) educational institutions can provide!

(The term western is used to distinguish it from the traditional teaching methods prevalent in the middle east and far east, including India where a teacher-student relationship is both personal and lifetime!)

However, the old traditional knowledge (skill-based, like pottery, priesthood in India) will then have an antique value which many of the in-between generations will struggle to adjust to socially. This is the Marxian nightmare superimposed on the Information Technology dominated world!

Will the regulative framework provide for higher and higher minimum standards of living in the developing world countries to keep its growing populations from spreading unrest?

As the starting point approaches the 1500 m race analogy, will succeeding generations be sufficiently occupied so that their minds are not diverted to the spread of destruction as a means of entertainment?

This question is best answered by those outside the domain of economics, typically those dealing with 'Purpose of Life' questions because such a domain only can keep mankind occupied once basic needs are satisfied over large periods!

Already the world is in a state where food production exceeds the food requirement of the entire population of the world! The problem is only by way of roadblocks to distribution and choice of the palate.

Soon, (meaning within the next 50 years) infrastructure needs will be sorted as per capita energy demands at a minimum level are bound to be met!

So, what do we do next? Go to the moon for a holiday? Sorry, Mr. Elon Musk is working on it already. Economics as a subject will perennially point to the income differential and pit man against woman keeping expectations at a level slightly above the minimum acceptable standard of living, no matter how high this is set in absolute terms.

Well, barely 150 years ago, we had no electricity and the income disparity was unbelievable at that time. Kings could afford to move food away from people so that it could be used in war elsewhere with exactly those people dying of hunger who toiled to produce it!

We are talking of the Bengal famine which happened as late as 1943! This might be difficult to replicate for any government in the future but the problem of lots of people with nothing to do can be more dangerous than the same number of people with nothing to eat. And that is why when the rich get richer and poor get richer above a minimum acceptable standard from an absolute point of view we need to pause for a cultural reset amongst all mankind!

6

real and unreal

One would expect the term 'real' to mean what is observed, isn't it? So, if you go to the market and ask for the price of potatoes and you are told it is Rs. 35/kg or 0.50 USD /kg, you are forgiven for thinking it is the 'real' price of potatoes!

Just, in case you thought, that I am accusing your vegetable vendor of cheating you then that is not the case. They too think it is the 'real price and they too are forgiven.

For the economists, the real value of the potatoes was what it was way back in the 1990s or say 10 years ago, that whenever they last went to the market and bought a basket of vegetables along with other household necessities!

Being the good mathematicians they are, they kept proper count of what they spent then and they argue that though potatoes may have gone up in price, something else in the basket of vegetables, say, carrots may have gone down in price by the same amount so on average the 'real' price remains unchanged!

So, I turned around to my professor and asked her then what is the price of Rs. 35/kg that is paid to the vegetable vendor called in their lingo, "Unreal?"

"Nominal" came the prompt reply. Well, now you know. Whatever you get in the market is always nominally priced! I bet all government spokespersons would love to quote this despite all the noises people may make about rising prices!

Befuddled at all this, I asked them (the economists, including myself) what this was all about only to get more confused with words and phrases like price index, normalized, base year, purchasing power, and inflation!

Ah! Inflation that word again. From the Big Bang to economics, this word seems to explain the true beginnings of everything, or should I say, how everything real grows?

In short, whatever I bought for a unit of currency in any country of the world in the 90s would probably be available in lesser quantity now for the same unit of currency. That is, its price would have inflated. In rare cases, if I get more 'bang for the buck' the price has deflated and if it is the same it is stagflation! (The entire drug industry, by the way, is stagflated – do watch The Economics of Drugs on Netflix, for detailed understanding).

But occasionally, the economist goes to the market and when they calculate with the prices they observe, it changes the base year. Perhaps, their spouse gives them a slightly altered shopping list which then puts the whole world in a tizzy because suddenly nations are richer or poorer! Suddenly, new governments are answering mismanagement of funds by previous governments without realizing that Caesar's wife had deemed so!

Now, this may to an extent offend you if you are an Economics person – like me! But this has come to me by varied arguments that I had with my friends and hence, this book – "An Outsider Looking In".

One thing for sure, if food prices don't vary much, people are clothed for the climates they are in and they all have some cozy place to spend their nights in, most of this discussion remains restricted to the process of normalization!

Herein, we enter a domain that many economists stay away from – econometrics!

Well, in an introductory class of econometrics, my professor once asked the class, what is the difference between mathematics and statistics, can someone explain with an easy-to-understand example?

After the usual commotion professor wrote two equations of a straight line on the board –

$Y = mx + c$ (1)

$Y = mx + c \pm \varepsilon$ (2)

'ε' the professor explained was 'error term'.

When one wants to calculate the location of points on a line, one can use the mathematical formula at 1, but when one plot (draws) a line that passes through a host of points as calculated by the mathematical equation on a graph and then looks at the line through a microscope then one finds that some of the points are marginally away from the line! The distance by which the points are away from the line is 'really' visible under the microscope and this is the error of the 'point' from the 'ideal' line (of ideal mathematically computed points)!

In cases, where there are only two points for drawing the line, and all other points of the observed data are close to the line, (technically called the 'best fit' line) equally distributed on both sides but not on the line, this error is tangible and the line is said to represent the 'normalized' slope represented by the points on an average!

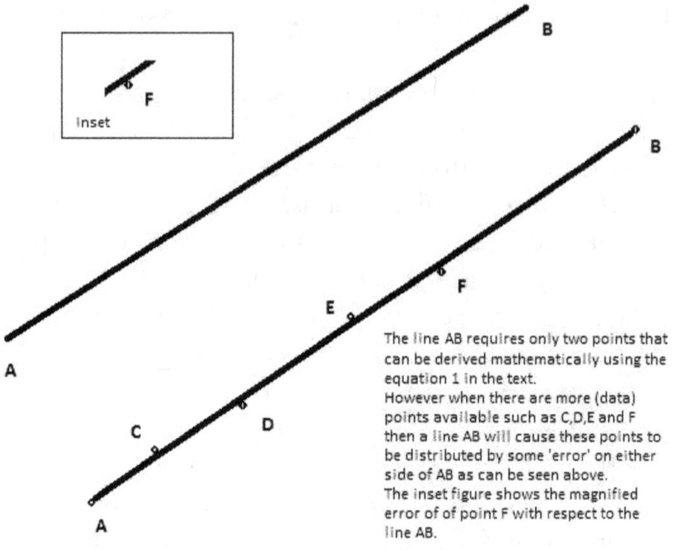

The line AB requires only two points that can be derived mathematically using the equation 1 in the text.
However when there are more (data) points available such as C,D,E and F then a line AB will cause these points to be distributed by some 'error' on either side of AB as can be seen above.
The inset figure shows the magnified error of of point F with respect to the line AB.

Figure 4 - How a straight line is differentiated in pure mathematics and statistics.

The reason for 'normalizing' or creating the best fit line from a host of data points is that it is the most reliable way to predict one data point that lies in between the extremes or extrapolate to one or two data points that are close to either extreme.

In short, normalizing, or linearizing helps to predict. Thus, many prices of every item of the basket in the 'shopping' list are normalized concerning, the quantity of purchase (obviously, even with your vegetable vendor, if you buy 1 kilo of potatoes and 100 kilos of potatoes there will be some negotiating margin. If nothing the store owner might agree to drop it at your home free of cost), area of transaction, (a country is a very large geographical spread, so prices vary), and of course, seasons (the time factor) to name a few variables!

The real, in economics, then, is anything but what it means to laypersons. It is highly contrived by statisticians who are so far away from reality and so close to numbers that they wouldn't know the normal ones from the sweet ones of the potato variety which, the prices on their graphs reflect!

So, it is with all statistics-based trade, the reality of senses and judgment is replaced by the surrealistic of numbers to decide the policies by which economies of the size of nations are administered. Numbers, as Pythagoras said, are all, in this area.

It gets more and more interesting when we turn to the most enticing of subjects in economics – the stock markets!

Here, it is, bizarre! Remember the sub-prime crisis? First, people with subprime creditworthiness are allowed to buy "real" estate with a mortgage loan. Then, while the bank still knows, that such debtors are unable to repay their loans, it goes ahead and creates papers which are in effect selling these loans to others who hope to get a first right on the monies, if and when they are returned by the original debtors. Then, these papers are bundled by mixing a couple or more loans and sold again by slicing them such that no one complete paper has a link to one piece of real estate. Then again and again, in a manner that would do the oldest profession proud. Finally, when it is no longer possible to contain the charade, the original debtor runs away leaving the property to the banks or to the subsequent owners of part of the papers to see what money they can recover from the house or the garden or whatever piece of real estate is left, if at all it existed in the first place after having paid a huge amount for what turns out to be a small fraction of the apportioned ownership that has been transferred!

Surreal, right? Not quite, just enter the world of derivatives, futures, and options, if you desire the adrenaline rush that compares with bungy jumping in the world of economics. There is nothing real about it! It is a straightforward prediction (gamble, bet) based on available data. Those who don't understand calculus certainly, have no idea about what is happening. And those that do have no idea of the link with the actual goods or company whose stock they may be betting on! All they are looking at is trends of past data, their imagined correlations with geopolitics, and of course a lot of cross-talk between fellow traders!

Rarely is a genuine prediction backed by math based on real data! If it is known that there is real data available somewhere, enough layers are created, to ensure that it doesn't reach the markets! Analysts, TV anchors, media experts, and pseudo-economists!

Why?

Because it is most easy to make money in a given system that is set in place by somebody who is already on top of a particular food chain, without upsetting the apple cart of hierarchy within that system. Everybody wins if they stay where they are relatively. Those lower in the food chain have to step over the shoulders of those above them to move up the hierarchy till they are wise enough to retire or die young as they grow too big for their shoes. The person on top of the food chain has the most brilliant mathematical mind(s) working for him (usually male, one wonders why one hasn't heard of a female Warren Buffet or a George Soros!)

Also, because of the factors mentioned in the previous chapter. The truly rich, the top of the food chain people, know more about what is important to be known in so far as money-making is concerned.

Thus, they know more or are better informed on the latest in molecular biology or renewable energy and are already invested in the best possible avenues of return both in the long and the short term.

Frightened?

Well, what is surrealism all about if one can't paint a scary picture. But do not be disheartened the next chapter on Innovation tells us why away from the prying eyes of the rich and famous, there is always something happening somewhere not because it is intended so but because that is its very nature!

7

innovation and economics

Again, the need to make simple starting definitions guides us to the fact that Innovation is best understood as 'Invention + Value'. Thus, for something to qualify as an innovation, it must not only have inventive value, it must also have fiscal value or monetary return! Therefore, innovation ties technology and economics, and this is as simple as it gets.

In the previous century, owing to the slowness of information travel, a mere invention was presumed to generate monetary value because of its novelty factor. However, with a rise in near-instant communication, any ordinary invention is easily replicable in all markets across the world and the effort of the inventor is not compensated by the monopoly of future sales!

Also, inventions are becoming tougher and tougher to come by because of the huge weight of developments already done and the absence of the newer foundations on which to base on them (remember that basic particle physics and the world view based on it hasn't changed since the 70s).

Therefore, we are a sort of mental stasis which is akin to the period post the development of the wheel!

Yet, relatively smaller breakthroughs agglomerate silently in unconnected areas and these provide avenues for scientists and engineers to think that they spur each other onto higher and higher levels of excellence.

A very crude example of this is the ratio of the weight of an automobile to the weight of its maximum human payload! In India or China, where this ratio is likely to be most efficient, an automobile weighs around 700 kgs and carries a maximum of 5 persons each weighing an average of 70 kgs, so this ratio should 0.5! We are hitting almost a peak in the weight of payload to the weight of the vehicle here. When only one person drives, which is mostly the case in the first world, this ratio is between 0.1 and 0.01 – a different order of magnitude!

Thus, when markets exist for different orders of magnitude of a fundamental metric in the same application, we can be sure that Innovation will thrive in that industry its economics can be predicted with some stability till an entirely new disruptor upsets the economic game.

The word disruptor is closely aligned to the concept of innovation. Generally, economics deals with data and prediction of the future based on past data. The most complex models are what is called the "transient response for a second-order differential equation" – in simple words, it is the minimum time in which a predicted response (or 99.8% to 100.2% of the predicted response) is achieved when any system is subjected to all its forcing functions. However, as with all things legal, science and engineering, too, have their finer points, or the small print, sometimes more so!

The small print is the term, 'feedback' and its general common representation in books of Modern Control Systems is given below –

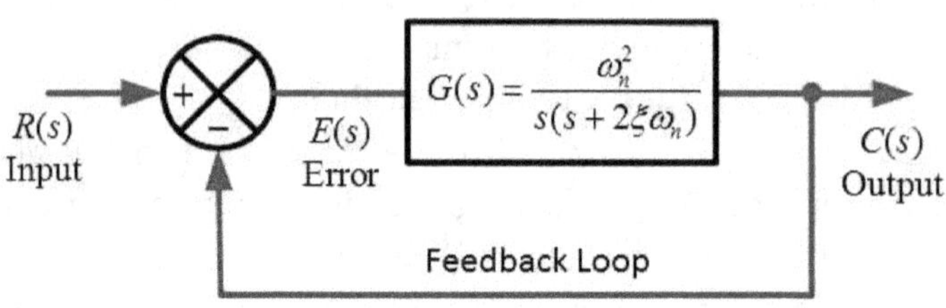

Figure 5 - A 2nd Order Control System Block Diagram

Don't bother about the equation in the figure above, but as an economist and partially less knowledge on Control Engineering author has derived an analogy from the same! The control system G(s), here is the economic system, that the economist aims to control to achieve a state denoted by the output C(s), after inputting R(s).

When C(s) does not reach its desired value, the economist adjusts the R(s) through the error function E(s) in the 'Feedback Loop', so that C(s) is attained by compensation. It does not matter what the G(s) is if R(s) can be adjusted to the till E(s)=0, and C(s) can be by and large controlled to desired values.

Why have we chosen a second-order control system, because that is the highest level of mathematics that we can handle presently!

And here comes the punch - The Innovation process, from an economic point of view, is essentially a Feedforward System – the arrow that is labeled feedback moves in the opposite direction! Essentially this means that the time in which the output is desired to settle within 0.2% of its predicted value is essentially unpredictable!

It is interesting to read Wikipedia on the basics of a feedforward control system to see if the authors hunch on the Innovation process being one such, is reasonably true or not –

A feed forward, sometimes written feedforward, is an element or pathway within a <u>controlsystem</u> that passes a controlling signal from a source in its external environment to a load elsewhere in its external environment. This is often a command signal from an external operator.

A control system that has only feed-forward behavior responds to its control signal in a pre-defined way without responding to how the load reacts; it is in contrast with a system that also has <u>feedback</u>, which adjusts the output to take account of how it affects the load, and how the load itself may vary unpredictably; the load is considered to belong to the external environment of the system.

In a feed-forward system, the control variable adjustment is not error-based. Instead, it is based on knowledge about the process in the form of a mathematical model of the process and knowledge about or measurements of the process disturbances.

(Haugen, F. (2009). Basic Dynamics and Control.)

The last paragraph has been particularly italicized because when it comes to the Innovation process the economist does not know as this is a very specialized area!

The entire article on Wikipedia was an eye-opener for the author who all along felt this connection in his gut!

Shorn of all engineering jargon, a feedforward system is a combination of man interacting with the machine in an open environment! The vagaries are just too much to model mathematically and what cannot be modeled mathematically is not the economists' domain, and here is where the innovation is the disruptor!

Going back to the metric of payload to the weight of an automobile, the other favorite metric of most Indians is the fuel/energy cost per kilometer. This disrupting metric is going to see Innovation thrive in the automotive sector driven by the energy storage technologies and the charging technologies that are made available unless lobbying prevents unfavorable regulatory frameworks that work in opposition to it.

Notwithstanding all that is written, many multinationals have systematized their approach as an organization to innovation in their chosen areas under the feedback control system like Bosch, Toyota, Apple, Samsung, and what have you!

Grassroot innovation however remains the domain of the solitary reaper (groups) and marches forward with tremendous advancements in varied fields like agriculture, construction, genetics, medicine, drug delivery, nanotechnology, photonics, quantum computing, etc., counting finally on the human intellect for a breakthrough, despite tons of data and automation available at their disposal in the view those looking from the outside in!

This also provides for local innovators to exploit local needs away from the prying eyes of the truly rich that we had talked about in an earlier chapter. Small innovation keeps a lot of the populace engaged and satisfied with a sense of achievement that their work contributes to the society that they live in. This then could be the saving grace of the doomsday scenario painted in the surreal ocean of economics that is manipulated by the large sharks!

In summary, economics is about an ability to predict and usually, this works in linear domains or domains that are under some sort of control.

Innovation on the other hand, while it promises economic value by pointing to the utility of its output, is an uncontrolled process by itself. Their relationship is at best tenuous, at worst it is stifling! Ask any person in Research and Development.

8
economics and culture

"Culture is an activity of thought, and receptiveness to beauty and humane feeling. Scraps of information have nothing to do with it. A merely well-informed man is the most useless bore on God's earth."

- Aims of Education by A N Whitehead.

We saw earlier that the economist and the truly rich for whom many economists, other than those with a passion for academics, work are extremely interested in information! It then seems Whitehead's view that they are bores of a high order!

Like economics, culture spans a wide spectrum and when the dust settles on a period of civilization that has tasted some prosperity and peace, we find that the investment in culture becomes both increased and refined.

While there may be many instances one can quote from the golden period of Indian history, universally acknowledged to be between the first and sixth centuries AD, it is more pertinent to be with the times.

So, what are the beacons of culture in today's India? The two words come to mind immediately, and both have a powerful economic bearing – Bollywood and Cricket.

Both appeal to the bottom of the large pyramid that is the South Asian population and the South Asian diaspora around the world, right up to the President of the largest Democracy in the world along with the volatile neighbors with whom India shares an intense love-hate relationship owing to a colonial past!

The root cause of this huge connection is the common medium of communication – the language! On the western front, Urdu and Hindi share a very large part of a common vocabulary and on the eastern front, it is the same language as Bengali.

Even in cricket, it is the huge spectator intercourse that sees sustained traction for the sport in a country that is otherwise reasonably poor in its all-around sporting performance.

Coming to economics, Bollywood and of course, the regional movie industry is a multi-billion-dollar concern and not to be taken lightly at all. Cricket on the other hand with its domestic league with two seasons in a year has a huge parallel economy in betting which makes one wonder as to how a country that looks for aid when it comes to child vaccination can have such a subaltern avenue for its spent!

Serious thought is given every year to regulate the betting industry associated with cricket on the lines of the Ladbrokes in the UK but year on year there is no movement on it. Perhaps, successive governments, too, carry on the hypocrisy of not allowing a 'sinful' pastime, but it is the authors' conviction that it has more to do with administrative and legal incapability to regulate the industry once the ball is set rolling!

This brings us to an important clarification about culture – in many places, the word culture is used for religion! Here, it is not.

But is there a connection between religion and economics? Surely there is and suffice it to say that in most religions lending on interest within the members of that religion is considered a sin. Thus, it is with Jews and so it is in all Islamic transactions without regard to the religious denomination of the other side!

For the rest, of course, economics in religion is like economics in any other temporal domain, strictly divorced from its spiritual message.

In Ancient India, this is slightly different. The approach is rather holistic and covered under what is called the "Purushaartha". It is a compound for two words, Purusha, meaning man, and Artha commonly translated as meaning, purpose, finance, and wealth concerning the sphere of activities that engage a person throughout their life!

Purushaartha is divided into four again –

Dharm Largely ethics

Arth Largely finance, wealth, but the deeper meaning is security

Kaam Desires and bodily needs

Moksh Freedom in the ultimate sense

Some philosophers do not consider Moksha as a Purushaartha, but this book isn't about philosophy so we can let that angle rest in peace. Our focus is on Artha and the guiding document on this a magnum opus called the Arthashaastra attributed to a giant among Indian intellectuals – Kautilya, more commonly known as Chanakya.

It is now getting acknowledged that the source for the pioneering work in Economics by Adam Smith called the Wealth of Nations may be Kautilya's Arthashaastra.

"It is almost a unanimously accepted view that The Wealth of Nations does not contain a single original idea establishing the fact that Adam Smith borrowed all key ideas from various sources. He believed that he could claim originality for all the important ideas if he concealed their sources. Ferguson exposed Adam Smith for making a false claim related to the pin-factory example. It is intended to continue the process initiated by Ferguson by identifying paragraphs on sources of economic growth, canons of taxation, and undesirability of monopolies, the core of The Wealth of Nations, which are textually quite similar to those in The Arthashaastra. It is claimed that Adam Smith lifted those ideas from The Arthashaastra. It is indicated in the Appendix that more than two hundred years before Adam Smith, Machiavelli also seems to have access to The Arthashaastra. Hopefully, this process continues until all of Adam Smith's sources are identified and duly acknowledged."

Kautilya's Arthashaastra: A Recognizable Source of the Wealth of Nations by Balbir Sihag

One reading of the contents of The Arthashaastra will tell us how it might shrink Sun Tzu's famed Art of War to insignificance. With this tremendous intellectual advantage through centuries, one must feel assured how millennia of the alien rule haven't yet completely made India intellectually and economically bankrupt!

We saw earlier that how every society might need a cultural bulwark that fortifies it against the vagaries of material progress that is measured by its economics!

When people have enough for their basic needs, it is an exploration of culture that lends stability to the economic system. One can see it in history through the golden age of the Indian subcontinent, the Islamic expansion that delivered critical know-how from the East to Europe, the renaissance in Europe itself, and the massive global impact of the industrial and technological revolution which now portends to take us into a future dominated by robots and artificial intelligence, leaving the man to explore finer and finer aspects of the wonderful creation that surrounds us – A mystery that deepens as we dig with greater intensity and to greater depths!

Towards the end, let us look at one last connection between culture and economics which happens through the bridge of standardization!

Any standard is anathema to a purist of culture. But mass appeal even in as individual afield as music comes only when standards apply. Thus, symphonies, melodies, ragas (the Indian classical music form of standard expression) bring the substratum of standards on which increasingly heightened levels of individual expression are trapped.

To take an example out of a favorite dining table conversation, the author was pleasantly surprised by a piece of information given to him by his colleague who had a passionate hobby in collecting chilies (the long vegetable variety of pepper) of varying degrees of hotness! It seems the hotness of chilies is measured on a standard scale called the Scoville Heat Units! Now the author was left wondering how the sensitivity of her father to the heat of chilies, which is expressed in form of tears, and her sensitivity which manifests as hiccoughs has been converted into a standard scale!

The answer is markets and economics that transports cultures from regions that were akin to remote islands onto every drawing room for understanding, choice, decision-making, and communication!

9
conclusion

As we round off, you might recollect reading that the author suggested a minimum set of subjects at the high school level to render an individual fit for society. The subjects were psychology, calculus, and an ancient language.

Towards the end of the book, the biggest takeaway for the author is that economics is probably not an undergraduate program but starts as a postgraduate course. Therefore, at an undergraduate level, the necessary foundations in the following subjects are required so that any holder of academic qualification in economics becomes a strong contributor to the society they live in –

1. Psychology
2. Language
3. Calculus
4. Basics of Law
5. Measurement (not limited to accounting)

While the first three, would have moved from a high school level to the undergraduate level, the introduction of the law might bring in an exposure to the preservation of ethics and virtue that is the hallmark of civilization.

Measurement is the basis of knowledge, at least in the material sphere. Exposure to this might give the student a width of view that enables them to combine inputs from other subjects on a common canvas.

The unit of economic activity is a transaction. This effect of a transaction in the economic sphere is much like the collapse of the wave function in determining the location of an electron! There is a discontinuity with every transaction and the next transaction stitches together the fabric of economics. There would be holes in this fabric. There would less fabric and more holes! Because economics has no laws of conservation!

Interestingly, this absence of conservation laws in economics provides a saving grace. To connect again with figure 3 of the Introduction, there seems a way out of a doomsday scenario that technology and therefore the science behind it that is constrained by conservation laws, portends for the future with an IT dominated, AI governed, robotic way of life. The figure below shows the umbrella surface 'progressing' in a 'synergy'. Because it moves in a manner so that it maintains its secular credentials to all 3 axes, it entitles all participants of the economic world order including the environment a minimum acceptable level for themselves.

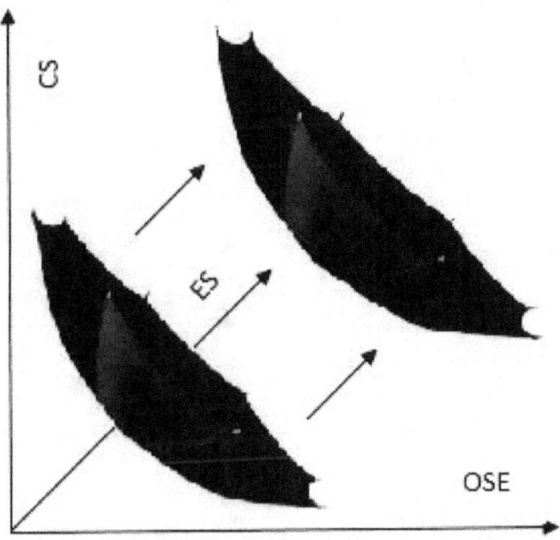

Figure 6 - The Direction of Synergy

It must be understood that this progression is not as neat as it looks because it is ideal. Therefore, it represents what is called a "process entitlement". But for the process entitlement to kick, a process needs to be defined, and in this case, the economic process needs complete definition the world over with each nation having the satisfaction of its people as its customer satisfaction, the government vision for that nation as the other stakeholder expectation and its agreed environmental obligations aligned to the respective axes.

Since none of these are tightly defined, the umbrella surface is highly distorted in reality to the extent of being torn and tattered at places. To make predictions difficult we have an emotional aspect of human beings cloaked under the rational pursuit of technology which makes economics such an enticing pursuit of a lifetime.

Epilogue

Money brings power and knowledge combined with information is the key to making money consistently. When this is combined with a free society, the rich get richer and the poor, too, start getting richer. While this might sound utopian, unless there is a cultural bulwark to society, economic progress is likely to unhinge large numbers of people into uncivilized behavior purely for entertainment. In Ancient Indian parlance, these are termed Aasuric or demonic tendencies!

Once basic needs are satisfied, following a self-defined minimum acceptable standard of living, it is difficult to justify the 'reality of economics'. Beyond this threshold, the mind will play tricks and all human passions, particularly greed is buoyed by economic success! Some human anchor at such times helps. This is typically an elderly person who is healthy in body and mind.

Innovation is an economic disruptor hence keenly watched by both the rich, the academics, the aspiring, and the government. While it appears obvious after the fact, innovation as a process is uncontrolled and at its core dependent entirely on human intellect!

At the crossroads of culture, economics, and the confused notion of culture which passes as religion in some parts of the world, are three words – belief, trust, and faith. Of these, under economics only trust matters. It is computable in terms of risk and so a corresponding cost. Thus, one can allow transactions to proceed with the need for referral on its basis, at the same one can impede every transaction on the very same basis!

Since risk most simply defined is a product of probability and cost of the impact of a decision, the risk number, in terms of money, is almost fully dependent on the risk taker's assignment (either personal judgment based or mathematical model based) of probability - a reflection of the trust any one party has on the other party!

This simple exposition of the relationship between trust and cost is rarely found in books on economics! A complicated explanation of this is studied popularly under a branch of economics by the name of 'Game Theory' and naturally, it models all the complicated situations that arise in real life as any proper pursuit of a branch of academics should. But, when we impart the academic content alone without making this simple basis clear, then we build castles on the weak foundation of what the student has grasped. A degree or diploma then only serves to bolster a false sense of knowledge which collapses when the weight of academics at the higher level becomes too much for the foundation. Culture is a huge economic driver in peaceful times as it engages the masses under a regulated framework and propels them to seek higher and higher thresholds of excellence in their chosen fields. It keeps people gainfully and satisfactorily employed without being a source of nuisance to one another!

The Indian way of life which apportions equal importance to Dharma (Ethics), Artha (security), and Kaama (Desire) seems to be the ideal framework that covers the complete spectrum of the future body of knowledge that modern economics might enlighten us on! For this the human aspects can be explored through the subject of psychology, the material aspects through the subject of calculus as modified by the results of measurement, and the communication of learning including changes to the required regulatory framework through language at the individual and the collective level.

In the future, it would be increasingly important for humans to spend prolonged periods doing nothing! How the economics of such a future state will pan out is anybody's guess! But for now, let us hope that this book inspires a lot of youngsters to study the subject, look at its impact on laypeople in their nations, propel all people wherever they are into higher and higher levels of minimum acceptable standards of living!